BEATING THE BLUES
This Holiday Season

Learn why the holiday season is a difficult time
of the year for many people, and what you can do to
help yourself and others

Bobbie Rill, M.A., LPC

The Grief & Wellness Group, Inc.
BobbieRill@gmail.com
www.TheGriefandWellnessGroup.com

Beating The Blues This Holiday Season
by Bobbie Rill, M.A., LPC
©2017 by Bobbie Rill. All rights reserved.

Copyediting of original version by
Adam and Ginger Colwell, Adam Colwell's WriteWorks, LLC

Revised cover and book interior design by
Carla Green, Clarity Designworks

Published by Adam Colwell's Write Works
via Kindle Direct Publishing and IngramSpark

Printed in the United States of America

ISBN (Paperback): 979-8-9914678-3-4
ISBN (eBook): 979-8-9914678-4-1

The information presented herein represents the view of the author as of the date of publication. Because of the rate with which conditions change, the author reserves the right to alter and update her opinion based on the new conditions/research. The article is for informational purposes only. While every attempt has been made to verify the information provided in this article, neither the author nor her affiliates/partners assume any responsibility for errors, inaccuracies, or omissions. Any slights of people or organizations are unintentional. If advice concerning legal or related matters is needed, the services of a fully qualified professional should be sought. This article is not intended for use in lieu of professional counseling.

I love to travel, but close to the holidays, the airports get a little harried. This trip was no exception, but I finally made my way on board the plane to Dallas, Texas with Tucson as my final destination, which has been my home for the last several years. After placing my briefcase in the overhead bin, I nestled into my seat by the window.

I've had my share of people climbing over me when sitting on the aisle. There was one time when the flight attendant was handing a woman her glass of beer, the woman inadvertently missed the cup and (you guessed it) the whole drink went all over me. From then on, it's been the window seat for me. I call the window seat my little corner of the world where, if necessary, I can bury myself in my latest John Grisham novel or entertain myself with Sudoku. I don't bother anyone, so I consider myself to be a great seatmate.

On this particular occasion, I was exhausted and decided to roll my jacket up, place it in the corner between the seat and the window, and plop my head in the middle of it in an attempt to get some rest as the final passengers found their seats. The man sitting in the aisle seat next to me seemed to get the message. After a brief greeting, he grabbed his *Wired* magazine. Although neither of us said a word, we silently hoped the middle seat would remain vacant.

Little did we know who was coming!

The woman, if I had to guess, was in her early to mid-forties. Perhaps she was well groomed earlier in the morning, but that certainly wasn't the case now as evening was setting in. She opened bin after bin as she came closer to our row. Then she opened the bin directly across from us, moved some items around, and hoisted up her oversized duffle bag, struggling with the weight of its contents. The gentleman on the aisle beside me jumped up to assist her. She thanked him and proceeded to make her way into the middle seat between us.

No doubt she had dragged that heavy bag through the terminal, working up a sweat and probably huffing and puffing along the way—at least that's what her disheveled appearance and ginormous sigh seemed to communicate. "Tough day?" I asked.

Words failed her momentarily, but the expression on her face and a nod said it all.

"Some rest will do you good," I offered as I nestled back into my corner and shut my eyes.

"Lord, help this woman," I prayed silently. "I don't know what her story is, but You do, and I really sense she needs Your help right now."

Although sleep evaded me, it felt good just to close my eyes for a few minutes. Doing that somehow seemed to help block out not only the sights but some of the sounds as well. Soon everything changed as the flight attendants made their way down the aisle with our beverage options. People readjusted themselves in their seats and the tray tables came down.

"Water for me," I spoke gently as the flight attendant leaned in. (I wanted to avoid caffeine in hopes of resuming my position in the corner and get some Zzzs.) My middle seatmate, who we'll call Jenny, ordered the same.

"Where are you headed," I asked Jenny, whose mind seemed to be miles away.

"Oh," she replied, "I'm on my way to visit my mom and stepdad. My sister and her kids will be there, too. It's been a while since I've been home, so I guess it will be good to see everyone."

That explained the heavy duffle bag. *Jenny is probably taking presents to everyone for Christmas, so she doesn't have to ship them. Smart idea,* I told myself.

Jenny and I continued our polite conversation, but when the gentleman on the aisle got up from his seat to use the restroom, Jenny seized her opportunity, making her way out of her seat and into the aisle where she opened the overhead bin and started rummaging through her duffle bag. I know it was probably not polite, but I couldn't help but notice that the bag was not filled with presents; far from it. Jenny had certainly been carrying a heavy load.

As I watched her toss aside a wrinkled blue blouse, a navy sweatshirt, a multi-colored scarf, and her blue pajamas, my mind drifted to the results of a survey I had read sometime before. It focused on what causes people the most stress during the holiday season. While I don't remember where I read it, three key results stuck in my mind.

1. **Being alone**

   Can you relate to this one? Most long to belong—to be loved and to love. Being alone for the holidays just doesn't seem right, and if you've lost a loved one or experienced the end of a romantic relationship, it can be downright unbearable.

2. Shopping and/or parties

Trying to decide what to get people is a major stressor, at least for me, not to even mention the financial strain. I want my gifts to be something useful, fun, and look extravagant, even if they are marked down 80 percent when I buy them! Guess my expectations on this one automatically sets me up for disappointment.

Then there's the parties! Personally, I like them. I love being with people and sometimes even acting like a complete fool. Yet I also know what it can be like if I'm not feeling especially social. So, in keeping with what we've been taught regarding what is socially acceptable, most of us will "put on a happy face" and act as though everything is fine!

Now, I've been a counselor for a long time, and if there's one thing I've learned, it's that F-I-N-E usually stands for Feelings Inside Not Expressed!

3. Being with family

How come being with the ones we love, or sometimes those who might be less than a loved one, causes so much stress? My mind jumped to a trip one summer to Disneyland. Without going into the details, let me just say I stood speechless as I watched two adult siblings engage in a rather loud argument in the middle of The Magic Kingdom.® At any rate, being with family can be extremely stressful, especially during the holidays.

Looking at Jenny and her current state, I wondered how she was going to navigate being with her family.

How easy it is to become overwhelmed by all the stress in life and the gamut of emotions that go with it. I continued to watch Jenny as she stuffed her blue garments back in her bag. My mind continued to wander. *Blue must be her favorite color,* I thought. But being near the holidays and observing Jenny, the color took on a different meaning. Wouldn't it be great if, instead of stuffing away all our hurts and disappointments—those things that cause us to feel blue—we could delve right into the recesses of our mind, pull them all out, and not just toss them aside but throw them away for good?

Then it hit me. There are many others just like Jenny. Maybe you're dragging a heavy, large, overstuffed duffle bag around. It's not a physical weight, though sometimes the emotional weight can feel like it's taking you to your knees. It's not something people can always see. After all, you've learned, just like the rest of us, to put on that happy face. 'Tis the season to be jolly, right?

Three important things came to me as I thought about the blues. First of all:

1. **Sad is real**

    In fact, S-A-D stands for Seasonal Affective Disorder. It's a very real thing many people struggle with. It is believed to have something to do with a lack of sun through which we take in Vitamin D. It's true that while people who live in gloomy areas are expected to be more susceptible to this, others in areas like Tucson, where we try to stay out of the sun for obvious reasons, are just as susceptible.

2. We've all experienced loss

While some of our losses may seem trivial, others are very significant. Interestingly, this time of the year stirs the pain of many of those losses. I wondered if Jenny had experienced the death of a loved one, a divorce, the loss of a job or moving, the loss of her home, or the death of a pet. There are over 40 different losses a person might experience during their life. I could only imagine that Jenny, like all of us, had already experienced multiple wounds.

3. People

Don't people (at least some of them) just drive you crazy? They just don't understand why the holidays can be so tough. No wonder! They have on their rose-colored glasses and are clueless just how difficult it can be for some; no, make that many!

So, how will you seek to beat the blues this holiday season?

A lot of people will try and white knuckle it so that they don't become extremely angry, or they might grit their teeth and struggle to get through it. But others may look for a way to relieve some of the built-up pressure by:

- Shopping, also known as retail therapy. Certainly, the holidays can give a person a great reason to max out those credit cards under the guise of Christmas shopping. But you know the truth! It's just a diversion to get your mind off your problems and try to elevate your mood.

- Baking. This keeps you busy and your mind occupied so you don't have to think about your pain.

- Eating. What is it with food? Remember eating the entire bag of potato chips? Cookies? Or _____? (Fill in the blank). The hope is to feel better, but you and I know we most often end up feeling worse.

- Drinking. Don't drink alcohol. Alcohol is a depressant and will exacerbate your feelings.

- Exercising.

- Movies, computers, TV, work...

You name it. There are tons of things you can use to try to avoid dealing with your hurt, disappointment, and all of those hopes and dreams that have never been realized. You can use just about anything to distract yourself from the pain so that you *think* it is working to relieve your stress and diminish your sadness. Eventually, though, you realize nothing has been resolved and once again, you're left with the pain.

I mentioned how we've been taught to put on a happy face. Stop and think about this for a moment. When did you start your acting career? Was it years ago? After the death of your son, your divorce, or the death of your mom? Have you become so good at pretending you're fine that you could be nominated for an Academy Award winning performance at church, at work, or in the presence of your friends? Like so many, when someone asks, "How are you today?" do you say you're fine? Great? Awesome?" Then, when you can no longer maintain the façade and someone asks, "What's wrong?" do you frequently find yourself replying, "Nothing?" Yet that's not what's going on inside. In fact, "nothing" could be further from the truth.

So, what is the truth? Let's look at these three items in a little more depth.

1. SAD IS REAL

There are many theories as to what causes Seasonal Affective Disorder (SAD):

- A decrease in serotonin.

- An increase in melatonin.

- A diminishing of light. One solution is to get more sunlight or, if you're in an area without direct sunlight, using light therapy.

I was recently reminded of that when several people I know put gorgeous sunrise photos on Facebook. I looked at those and thought, *I need to get out more.* I get up at 5:30 a.m. every day but can become glued to a computer right away. You, Jenny, and I all need 20 minutes of sunlight every day. For those of you who have or want to strengthen your faith, don't forget, Jesus said, "I am the Light of the World."

The other thing that helps with SAD, as well as when struggling with feelings of depression throughout the year, is exercise. Schedule 20 minutes a day for four days each week on your calendar, and make it a point to keep those appointments. Sometimes it can be hard because you lack the motivation. I know. But get up and get moving anyway.

Eating right is also important. Be careful not to overindulge in all the goodies offered, especially during this time of year. In fact, overindulgence might be one of your family traditions, so be sure to watch those habits closely. Remember the Garden of Eden? Satan used food to tempt Eve, and I'm convinced food is a great temptation for a lot of us!

Believe me, I know this is a lot easier said than done, but you need to do it in spite of how you feel. You must make decisions that you know are good for you. Like Nike says, "Just do it!" You don't want to make decisions based on how you feel at a time like this.

An Important Sidenote about Emotions

Emotions aren't positive or negative—they just are. When you go to any kind of buffet, you have a wide variety of choices: cold, hot, sweet, and sour. There are some flavors that are more palatable and others you don't care for at all. Maybe you don't even like the texture of some of the options before you.

Our emotions are like that buffet. They are the taste buds of life! Emotions are not good or bad. It's what you do with them that is important and determines whether the consequences will be positive or negative.

Take love for example. Love has a reputation of being this warm, fuzzy feeling, yet you can probably think of many occasions when love misdirected has had devastating consequences. Then there's anger. The message often given regarding the feeling of anger is that you *shouldn't* be angry. Right? Yet, Mothers Against Drunk Driving (MADD) is an organization that was established because the energy that came with anger (and there's a lot of energy with anger) was properly channeled and the results were powerful. Laws were established to help prevent people from driving on our roads and highways while under the influence of alcohol.

I think you get the idea. Emotions are not good or bad, positive or negative. It's what you choose to do with them—how you choose to *manage* your emotions—that's important.

Seek Professional Help

Throw away the notion that you can handle it on your own. If you fell and broke your leg, you wouldn't even give a second thought about going to the doctor. Do the same with your emotions. Call a mental health professional you trust who can offer understanding, insight, and is willing to walk you through this journey. You don't have to go through it alone.

2. WE'VE ALL EXPERIENCED LOSS

- End of a relationship
- Death of a loved one
- Death of a not-so-loved one (Frequently this might be an ex or a critical or abusive spouse or parent.)
- Loss of confidence
- Death of a pet

- Loss of hope
- Loss of a child
- Infertility
- Empty nest
- Loss of expectations
- The list goes on…

Don't be surprised. Even with an ex-spouse, when they die, you will grieve. You may wonder, *What is going on?* You might even think, *I should be glad the person is gone and out of my life!* In fact, you might feel both glad and sad, relieved and angry. Grief involves a whole gamut of different emotions. No matter what the loss is, it's important to know conflicting feelings can co-exist when you are grieving.

Learn to Grieve

Grief is emotional—not intellectual. That's why people may drive you crazy. They want to intellectualize grief, to get you out of your feelings and back in your head, so they can feel better.

Holidays, birthdays, and anniversaries can bring pain and regrets to the surface. We call these "triggers" that remind you of unresolved grief. There are a whole host of things like places, people, dates, songs, objects, and even smells that can trigger your brain, which has recorded everything that has ever happened to you, and flood your mind with the memories surrounding a past event.

When you think (intellectualize), you have trouble understanding and ask yourself, *What is wrong with me? Why can't I just get over this?* It's not what's wrong with you. It's that you need correct information on how to resolve your grief and a trusted individual to walk you through the process. Sometimes you are blessed to have good support because you have friends who will listen to you. That helps for a while, but take caution. You need to take specific steps for recovery. Not everyone knows what those steps are or how to guide you through the process. In fact, some people may give you bad advice.

An additional thought before we move on to the well-meaning (or not so well-meaning) people in our lives. Carrying around weights can be beneficial. Small, hand held dumbbells, for example, can build your muscles and even your endurance. While it's nearly impossible to see any good coming out of emotional weight and the painful situation or significant loss that comes with it, I'm impressed with the countless number of people who have allowed the tragedies in their lives to be used for good.

After the death of his infant son, John James began a journey to find help. Because of going through his pain after various attempts to avoid it failed, John became determined to find answers, so he could move on with his life. He eventually founded The Grief Recovery Institute and developed *The Grief Recovery Method* that has helped thousands recover from their losses, including the loss of a child. You can get through your loss—and when looking back, I hope you, too, will be able to say that not only has the weight of your pain diminished, but that you are better equipped to help guide others who need hope and a positive direction because of what you've been through.

3. PEOPLE

Let's face it! Some people drive us crazy. They, like us, have been taught to intellectualize grief. They do that because they don't know what to do or say to you when you are in pain. Tears and pain make most of them feel uncomfortable.

Grief Is the Result of a Broken Heart

Have you ever opened your heart to someone and shared honestly about a hurt in your life only to have the person you're talking to try to change the subject? I have. They often try to intellectualize your pain with words like, "Don't worry. You'll get through this," or "You're young enough to find another man...have another child...get another job." One woman who had two husbands die (one from cancer and the second from a heart attack) was told after the death of her second husband, "You'll be all right. You've been through this before."

Sometimes, people in our churches will add a story or verse from the Bible they hope will be a source of encouragement, help you accept what has happened, and cause you to move forward. Some of the frequent comments grievers in church have heard include, "God won't give you any more than you can bear," or "You know, God works all things together for the good of those who love Him," or "You just need to have more faith."

While there may be a lot of truth in some of those statements, people who are grieving say that those comments *aren't* what they need or even want. Some have even gone so far as to reveal that they wanted to smack the person.

Grief is not intellectual. Grief is the result of a broken heart—and that's what you need the people in your life to understand. You want people to accept your emotions. You need them to understand that your emotions are not a barometer of your faith or lack of it, but rather an expression of your grief.

Then There's You

Despite what you want or need from people, sometimes you can feel like a doormat. Maybe the people in your life walk all over your feelings because they don't know how to respond to what you're going through. But perhaps you can be your own worst enemy by beating yourself up, saying or thinking things like, "What's my problem?" or "I shouldn't be crying," or "I should be over this by now."

You're not a doormat for yourself or others to walk on. Remember when women went outside and hung their rugs over the clothesline or fence to beat them? Consider taking the end of a broom, or better yet, a bat—and BEAT THE RUG, not yourself! Put some action behind those emotions. Let it out!

Self-talk

Watch what you're thinking about and how you refer to yourself in your thoughts. You may tend to be hard, critical, or judgmental.

Here's a little exercise. Right now, get a pen and write down three personality characteristics that you love about yourself. (Such characteristics can include outgoing, spontaneous, loyal, knowledgeable, gorgeous, funny, brave, dedicated, honest, talented, or fearless.)

1. _____

2. _____

3. _____

Now, find a mirror in your home and look at yourself. Tell yourself these three things out loud. It might feel silly, but do it anyway.

Start focusing on these strengths and immediately spot any *stinkin' thinkin'* you might find yourself drawn to during your grief. Stop telling yourself you must be strong, keep busy, and just give it time. Those are lies that will not help you. Above all, don't become one of those people who drive you crazy.

Finally, let out that primal scream if you need to. Some say it helps. I remember a young married woman in her late twenties who said she was really having a bad day, so she put her child in the play pen, went out in her garage, and just let out a loud scream. She felt much better. A few days later when over at a neighbor's house for coffee, the friend asked if she had heard a woman scream. She did not confess it was her, but nonetheless decided she had best not do that again, or at least she should go somewhere out of hearing distance of her neighbor.

Here are two final personal solutions that can help.

1. ACCEPT that your feelings are okay

People don't understand that sadness is just as appropriate in a painful situation as a joyful feeling in a happy occasion. Let's say a young couple just announced to a big group that they're engaged. If I went up to them and said, "Don't be happy. Don't you know that fifty percent of marriages end in divorce?" They'd likely think that was a horrible thing to say, and they'd maybe even have the courage to confront me. They'd also think I was crazy or worse.

But how many times have you had someone say, "Don't be sad," or "Don't cry about..." after a pet died? No matter what people might say, begin to be okay with your feelings. Accept them. Most of them are the very normal and natural expression of your grief, but that doesn't give you a license to be cruel to others. You are responsible and need to take responsibility for what you say and do.

2. RECOGNIZE that your tears are acceptable

We've been trained to hide our tears and swallow most of our emotions. Ask yourself, *What would happen if people saw my tears? Might they think I'm out of control?* We want people to think we are strong and that we can handle anything. Image is so important in our culture.

Remember, your tears are okay, and there really is a benefit to a good cry. I know we've all been taught to wipe our tears away, but you don't have to! You can let them roll down your cheeks if you'd like. Also, if you see someone crying as they tell you about their broken heart, you can have Kleenex handy, but don't hand them one. That might continue to convey the message they've gotten all their life: tears are bad and need to be wiped away. Let people know tears are okay in your presence, and let your own tears be okay with you.

I saw a picture with a saying that I really liked. It showed a camera. The words said, "Just focus on what's important. Capture the good times. Develop from the negatives, and if things don't turn out...just take another shot."

• • • • •

After Jenny found what she was looking for in her duffle bag, she climbed back into her seat. "Excuse me," she said, "but can I ask you a question?"

Before I could respond, Jenny opened the folder she was holding, pulled out two airline tickets, and began to tell me her story.

I had just prayed for God to help this woman. Now, I realized I needed to be willing to give up a few Zzzzs to listen to Jenny without judgment, criticism, or analysis. I needed to be a heart with ears. **A heart with ears.** That's what a grieving person wants and needs!

"Six months ago, my husband of 15 years died," she began.

"What happened?" I asked.

"We had always wanted to go to Hawaii. We talked about it for years—the honeymoon we never had but kept putting off because of finances. Finally, we made the plans, and shortly afterward, he had a heart attack after his regular morning run. He hadn't felt good the night before, but neither of us thought anything about it. He chalked it up to indigestion," she said.

"I don't get it," Jenny continued with a surge of emotion. "We ate right, and he exercised regularly. I've been a wreck ever since. I just don't know what to do with myself or these tickets to Hawaii."

"That's quite a dilemma," I replied. "I can't imagine what your life has been like these last months."

Jenny began to cry. "It's been hell, to be honest," she said through her sobs.

I just let Jenny cry and validated her feelings as was appropriate as she spoke about her husband's death. He was her best friend, her lover, her confidant, her encourager, and her life. She went on to talk about her loneliness and the regret of not taking the trip to Hawaii.

I explained that grief is almost always about significant emotional communications that, for one reason or another, were never delivered or perhaps never heard. In Jenny's case, she never had the opportunity to tell her husband one last time that she loved him or to apologize for suggesting repeatedly that they postpone their trip. While Jenny would never be able to tell her husband those things, I gave her a heart with ears that day that I hoped would help her—and fulfill the prayer I had spoken about her.

As the plane landed, Jenny took her duffle bag out of the overhead bin with the help of the gentleman sitting on her other side. She still had a lot of things to ponder, including gifting the airline tickets to Hawaii to her parents or younger sister and her husband, but her load seemed just a little lighter.

We hugged as we parted ways.

Hopefully, Jenny's holidays will include a whole host of wonderful memories she and her husband had made together amidst her sadness.

Whatever the cause of your holiday blues, I wish the same for you.

A Final Word from Bobbie

The survey cited earlier reported that being alone during the holidays is hard and the number one cause of stress for people—but you can be with a crowd of individuals and still be very lonely. The loneliness may be hidden behind a mask as a means of pretending everything is fine while you stuff the pain and hope someday the hurt will go away. Don't forget. Time doesn't heal all wounds. Taking the appropriate steps can take you through your grief.

Through the Grief and Wellness Group, Inc., I have the honor of helping people work through their grief whether it's been recent or years ago. One woman recently told me, "This is the first time in two years that I have smiled. Not the plastic smile—I mean the smile from within." After completing her grief recovery, she could experience freedom and say goodbye to the pain.

No matter what your losses have been or how long ago they occurred, there is help. Look for a Grief Recovery Specialist® in your area. In the Tucson area, please give us a call at The Grief & Wellness Group, Inc., 520-668-5906.

ABOUT THE AUTHOR

Bobbie Rill, M.A., LPC

Bobbie is the Southern Arizona Clinical Director of the Arizona Family Counseling Center, a ministry of Christian Family Care. She has been a Licensed Professional Counselor for over 30 years focusing on relationship dynamics, common mental health issues, and is a Certified Clinical Trauma Professional. In addition, she is an Advanced Certified Grief Recovery Method Specialist and National Trainer of Trainers for the Grief Recovery Institute.

Her background includes serving as the Executive Director of a multi-state network of counseling centers where she supervised a staff of 50 including both Master and Doctorate level therapists. She is a frequent event speaker and has been a guest on numerous radio shows.

Prior to Bobbie joining the CFC staff, she and her husband, Bob, founded The Grief & Wellness Group in Tucson, AZ.

They have two married, adult children, two adorable grandkids, and a German Short Hair dog, all of whom keep them on their toes.

Bobbie Rill, M.A., LPC
Grief Recovery Specialist® and National Trainer
The Grief & Wellness Group, Inc.
www.TheGriefandWellnessGroup.com
BobbieRill@gmail.com
520-668-5906